INTERFERENCE

How the Baylor Sex Assaults Shed Light on Faith and Football

by Laura Leigh Majernik

COPYRIGHT

*This book is dedicated to
Jane Does 1-15:
I hear you,
I believe you,
I pray for you.*

INTRODUCTION

December 27, 2018
NRG Stadium
Houston, TX

As I waited for Baylor Bears head coach Matt Rhule to join the postgame press conference, I fought the urge to sleep. Baylor emerged from the Academy Sports + Outdoors Texas Bowl as the victors over Vanderbilt. But with an 8 p.m. kickoff time, that meant the postgame press conference took place after midnight. Despite the late hour, there was no way I was going to miss a press conference with Baylor's coach and a few of its players.

The wait time gave me a moment to muse over the irony of covering Baylor football. When I earned credentials to this bowl game, my emotions were mixed. Covering bowl games brings an air of festivity unlike the regular season, so I looked forward to that, but...*Baylor*.

Baylor, indeed. The football team that led me down a two-year path of research, then into the whole terrible saga of the sexual assaults on campus. The school that has a major Title IX trial pending against it. I wanted to hear from today's Baylor team, though. Additionally, I realized this was the best time to cover the team -- at the end of the journey into what took place on campus.

At last, Coach Rhule appeared; the man who took on the head coaching job after Art Briles left the program following the assault revelations. *(Note: Jim Grobe served as Interim Coach for the first season after Briles's departure).* I tried to keep a balanced perspective on Rhule while he spoke to the media.

By the end of the press conference, Coach Rhule had impressed me. His passion for the game equals his commitment to his players. Quarterback Charlie Brewer, who also attended the press conference, addressed the media with a sincerity and humility beyond his years. With a man like Rhule coaching young men like Brewer, the future for Baylor football looks bright.

"I like him (Coach Rhule)," my friend and fellow media member, Mark, stated as we walked to the parking lot after the press conference.

"I do, too!" I gushed. "In fact, I think I just added a chapter to my book...oh, the irony!"

How could I possibly like anything to do with Baylor football after everything I learned about Baylor?

It was because I knew football had very little to do with what happened.

HOW I FOUND THE BAYLOR STORY

BAYLOR IN THE HEADLINES

My "Baylor obsession" began in August 2015 after reading a *Texas Monthly* article about sexual assaults allegedly committed by two Baylor football players.[1] At the time, I hosted a podcast and wrote blog articles on college football and my social media feeds consisted of updates on teams and players. However, this story hit me harder than similar scandals which unfortunately permeated sports headlines.

What made Baylor's tragedy different? For me, their status as a private Christian school. Baylor University prides itself on its Baptist roots. I expected a school with a commitment to Christian principles to make every effort to comfort the hurting and seek justice where needed.

Few details were available during the 2015 football season. Finally, in February 2016, the whole terrible saga made its way to the public through ESPN's "Outside the Lines."[2] And the story was even worse than I feared: there were more incidents of sexual assault than initially reported, and while football players allegedly committed some of the crimes, some non-athletes were also receiving scrutiny.

The university's treatment of the victims surprised me. University personnel allegedly reacted to claims made by the victims with a dismissive attitude. Survivors of a violent crime sought support from their university, but no support appeared to be given to help them recover from their trauma. Why did Baylor fail to provide support in an atmosphere of Christian compassion?

Baylor failed because any university will conceal criminal behavior in the interest of worldly success. Even a university that prides itself on its Christian values.

What makes this book different from other books on the sexual assaults that happened at Baylor? It looks beyond football. While football brought the story to the public, it's a small part of a bigger picture. Looking at the situation from a Christian focus also provides a different perspective in this work. Women experience sexual assault, even at Christian universities. Therefore, they deserve the accommodations as stated in the law, particularly Title IX. Christ-centered care should be the added layer of compassion when an assault happens at a Christian university.

The results of my look into Baylor's sex assaults follow. I want you to understand one main point: *What happened at Baylor was about more than football.*

WHAT I LEARNED ABOUT COLLEGE FOOTBALL AND MONEY

THE MONEY-MAKING MEAT GRINDER

College football provides a fun hobby for many people. Watching one's alma mater win games gives us an ego boost. The players do the hard work, but we all take the credit and bask in superiority for the season. The flip side, watching our team lose game after game, gives us the blues. Ironically, we shift blame when our team loses as quickly as we take credit for their winning. Blame the coach, or the player who missed a tackle or threw an interception; that's how we cope with loss.

That's only one side of the picture. Underneath the swagger of players and coaches lies the reality: college football is a business. I call it the Money-Making Meat Grinder. Bigger programs, the ones that have large fan bases, make hundreds of thousands of dollars for their schools. The winning schools attract more applicants: students want to align with winners. Coaches receive incredible salaries, and games unfold in stadiums with state-of-the-art locker rooms and training areas.

This opulence is paid for by the labor of late teen and early twenty-something young men. In return, these men earn a college education, free room and board, and the chance for glory. Hopefully, some players find themselves on NFL rosters once their college days are over. That is, if there are no career-ending injuries or offseason shenanigans.

Digging through this business side of college football made me look at the game differently.

Money is the Real Goal

Anyone who takes a minute to do a simple search online will learn that college football makes a lot of money. The results from my own quick search rendered me speechless.

Several books explain the business of college football. Inevitably, any book that pulls back the proverbial curtain on a revered tradition exposes the reader to some harsh realities. Namely, this section of sports literature shows the reader that what happens on the field is arguably the smallest part of what makes up college football.

The System: The Glory and Scandal of Big-Time College Football by Jeff Benedict and Armen Keteyian gave me the best overview of the game. The authors manage to give an up-close look of several major programs and even spend time on some of the controversies. It allowed me to see how Baylor fit in the current football climate.

The purpose of college football was the biggest lesson I learned from *The System*. It's not to bring alumni and current students together to cheer for their school. Serving as a training ground for future NFL stars plays some role in why schools field teams. But at the sport's core lies one thing: making money.[3] Teams bring in money to their schools. Television contracts provide millions of dollars to the nation's biggest programs. In addition, the more successful a team, the more money its alumni donate to the school. Alumni want to keep up the school's reputation, which is judged more by football prowess than academic success.

With so much money on the line, the team must win. The top players do their best to excel every week. No room exists for injury, especially for a scholarship athlete. "Playing through the pain" is commonplace. Injuries can also affect a player's NFL prospects. Professional teams are unlikely to draft an injury-prone player. And, unfortunately, some players suffer career-ending injuries. Their dreams of money and fame in the NFL disappear in an instant.

Students and fans view these players through superhero lenses. The wide receiver who catches the winning pass in the final seconds for the upset win appears to walk on water the following week on campus. And when these players are elevated to this status, it makes them feel like rock stars. They're given special treatment by those around them because they are *special* – not just any twenty-year-old man can hurdle over his opponent as he speeds to the end zone.

Admiration of a player's skill is not objectionable. When that admiration moves to idolizing, though, then there's a potential for problems. A player starts to believe he can push any boundaries, *on or off the field*. Those boundaries include the law, as is alleged in several cases at Baylor. If a young person believes the world exists to do his bidding, he may not know how to accept a young woman saying," No" to his overtures. He's a star. He can take what he wants in any case – without any consequences.

The school that sees him as a valuable investment may also be more likely to look the other way if he happens to break the law. They need him to play to bring in the attention that results in money.

From X's and O's to "Yeses" and "No's"

With her appropriately titled *Saturday Millionaires*, Kristi Dosh, aka "the Sports BizMiss," produced an interesting work on the impact of football on a school's bottom line

Guess what? It turns out that a school's football success plays a role in the number of admission applications the school receives. I spoke about this on my podcast and had the privilege of interviewing Dosh as well. The reality of sports programs' economic impact is phenomenal.

In her book, Dosh explains how a sports team serves as a form of advertising for a school (and if you watch games, you'll even see promotion pieces for the schools competing in the game), but the best-known advertising impact on admissions is called "The Flutie Effect."[4]

Those of you who are old enough will remember that game; I sure do. It was 1984, and Boston College quarterback Doug Flutie threw a last-second "Hail Mary" pass that was caught in the end zone. The resulting touchdown meant a victory for BC over the University of Miami and sealed a Heisman Trophy win for Flutie. That dramatic game winning pass *also* resulted in a thirty percent increase in applications to Boston College for the next year. *Thirty percent!* Thus the name, "The Flutie Effect."[5]

When a football team posts a winning season, the

Flutie Effect still occurs today: an uptick in applications follows. It may also drive an increase in donations and government funding, and in some instances, a higher ranking for the school in the all-important *US News and World Report* rankings results.[6] The positive effect cannot be overstated.

A team's level of success also makes a difference. Devin G. Pope and his brother and fellow economist, Jaren C. Pope, found that winning a national championship increases applications seven to eight percent.[7] The increase doesn't last forever, but the studies have noted a lifespan of three application cycles experiencing it.[8]

More applications lead to more students, leading to more tuition dollars for some schools. In other cases, schools find the increased applicant pool allows for more selectivity in admissions. Either way, this increase in applications cannot be duplicated by even the very best public relations campaigns.

Dosh gave more underpinning of the positive effects a successful football team brings a university. Not only do more students apply, leading to bigger or more academically-sound freshman classes, but more students remain as well. One study concluded that "for each 4 percent increase in winning percentage they found a correlating 1 percent increase in graduation rate."[9] *Note: The study took place over a ten-year period.*

Beyond applications and retention, football success brings revenue. The previously mentioned increases in state funding for public universities and increased donations for public and private universities represents a portion of the money a school receives.

Then ticket sales bring in funds[10] as well as licensing.[11] Once you bring media rights revenues in the picture, the amount of money a school makes skyrockets, particularly for the schools with the biggest and most successful football programs.

This look at the positive aspects of a football program on a school underscores what happens when the football team succeeds. Negative effects also exist, but this work will not enumerate them beyond the example of a culture of tolerating violence on campus.

WHAT I LEARNED ABOUT COLLEGE SPORTS AND VIOLENCE

A DIFFERENT STANDARD

Jessica Luther literally wrote the book on violence in college sports. I had the privilege of interviewing her on my podcast in the spring of 2016, shortly before her book *Unsportsmanlike Conduct* hit the shelves. Luther, along with her colleague Dan Solomon, broke the watershed article about what was happening at Baylor for *Texas Monthly*.

Reading through *Unsportsmanlike Conduct* proved difficult, but it provides solid information. An especially relevant item from Luther's book pertains to student-athletes and how their cases of assault undergo different adjudication procedures than non-athletes. Luther writes:

> "In a July 2014 US Senate report titled, "Sexual Violence on Campus: How Too Many Institutions Are Failing to Protect Students," it was revealed that, "many institutions also use different adjudication procedures for student-athletes. More than 20 percent of institutions in the national sample give the athletic department oversight of sexual violence cases involving student-athletes. Approximately 20 percent of the nation's largest public institutions and 15 percent

of the largest private institutions allow their athletic departments to oversee cases involving student-athletes."[12]

The practice of athletic departments deciding punishments for student-athletes who commit assaults extends far beyond any one school you read about in the media. Unfortunately, the concept of holding athletes to different standards appears to be the norm on many campuses as well.

Given the relatively recent date of the U.S. Senate study (2014), it remains possible that campuses still conduct business this way. Schools' athletic departments carry out the coaching and training of athletes; adjudicating criminal behavior lies beyond their scope of operations.

Ironically, the increase of reports in these cases and this double standard makes it possible to change how campuses conduct their procedures. This is no longer a secret, and campuses likely want to avoid the negative publicity that other schools, such as Baylor, received.

WHAT HAPPENED AT BAYLOR

The Overview

College football makes money and improves admissions. College athletes who allegedly commit crimes are held to a different standard of adjudication. What does that have to do with Baylor?

Here's one way of looking at it, from the Bible, no less:

"For the love of money is a root of all kinds of evils. It is through this craving that some have wandered away from the faith and pierced themselves with many pangs." 1 Timothy 6:10 (ESV)

For a quick laic interpretation: Baylor lost their focus on Christ when they sought money and notoriety on the national level. Successful football teams, described in Dosh's work, provide a fast track to more money from tuition and donations. Beautiful McLane Stadium provides the most obvious example of the success of increased donor support based on football. The new facility appeals to recruits who will want to play for the Baylor Bears and keep the team successful, which brings in further donations and support from other avenues.

Unfortunately, the effect of this new focus left students who needed care after experiencing sexual assault without the assistance they sought and further devastated them. Several students brought lawsuits against the university for this lack of care. Some have been settled, but one suit, featuring ten plaintiffs known as "Jane Doe 1-10," is scheduled for October 2019.[13] The courts will then decide what restitution, if any, will be made for those who claim they were hurt.

An external investigation of the university's policies showed a glaring deficiency in how they handled cases of assault. The Pepper Hamilton law firm made recommendations for new policies, which were put in place.

However, making new policies doesn't mean the problem is solved, especially if the cultural attitude of minimizing victims' trauma remains the same. The cultural attitude of the campus, as displayed by the university's leadership, remains at the core of what happened at Baylor. If that does not change, the policies are nothing more than words on paper.

What Started the Investigation?

The case of Sam Ukwuachu led to Pepper Hamilton's investigation of the school. Ukwuachu, who never played a game for Baylor, became a part of the team after transferring from Boise State University in 2013. He sat out the 2013 per NCAA transfer rules. But when training camp began in the summer of 2014, he was suspended from the team instead of attending camp. Ukwuachu's suspension came after a June 2014 indictment on two counts of felony sexual assault. That conviction was later overturned, and he awaits a new trial.

Luther and Solomon's watershed, August 2015 *Texas Monthly* article discussed the Ukwuachu, as well as the Tevin Elliott, case.[14] Elliott was found guilty of felony sexual assault in January 2014 and now serves a twenty-year prison sentence.

Once light was shed on the situation, Baylor could no longer remain silent. In the fall of 2015, then-University President Ken Starr announced that an internal investigation would be launched on how the Ukwuachu case was managed by the university.

While conducting the investigation, law professor Jeremy Counsellor found that Baylor needed a more thorough examination of its handling of sexual assault cases. This in-depth investigation also required the work of an outside firm. Counsellor made these recommendations to Starr, who then engaged Pepper Hamilton.

The Pepper Hamilton law firm specializes in Title IX cases and works with universities across the country on implementing procedures for compliance with the law. The firm's goal for Baylor was reviewing Title IX responses to sexual assault allegations in a collection of test cases. After reviewing the cases, Pepper Hamilton would present its findings to Baylor's Board of Regents and make recommendations for improved procedures for future cases.

Baylor appeared to give the firm full access to the information it sought. No documents or interview subjects were off-limits. Pepper Hamilton began its work in September 2015 and announced to the Board of Regents in April 2016 that it had enough information to make recommendations. By May 2, a small committee of regents met with Pepper Hamilton for a preliminary briefing.

The discussion of the findings in the preliminary briefing hinted at such a serious lack of Title IX compliance that the group decided the regents needed to meet quickly as a whole to further discuss the findings.

The complete Board of Regents met on May 11 and 12 to hear a verbal presentation of Pepper Hamilton's findings. The presentation surprised the Board, as they claimed they were not aware of the deficiencies in Baylor's Title IX compliance and the upsetting details of the cases that the firm examined.

What is Title IX, Anyway?

From the Department of Education website:

"Title IX protects people from discrimination based on sex in education programs or activities that receive Federal financial assistance. Title IX states that:

No person in the United States shall, on the basis of sex, be excluded from participation in, be denied the benefits of, or be subjected to discrimination under any education program or activity receiving Federal financial assistance." Source: https:// www2.ed.gov/about/offices/list/ocr/docs/ tix_dis.html

We tend to think of Title IX in terms of funding for women's sports. However, it also protects students from a hostile environment in educational institutions. If a student reports sexual assault, the campus is required to make accommodations for that student to still receive an education. These accommodations can include changing a class schedule or receiving a grade of "incomplete" instead of a failing grade for a semester due to the extenuating circumstances of suffering trauma from the assault.

Survivors from Baylor attempted to access these accommodations and were not satisfied with the treatment they received from the university. By suing for the infringement of their rights under Title IX, the survivors have an opportunity to receive some adjudication for the way they were treated. These actions take place in civil, not criminal, court.

What Did the Report Say?

No "Pepper Hamilton report," *per se*, exists. Instead, the law firm gave a verbal presentation. The Board of Regents, in turn, released a "Findings of Fact," outlining the scope of the Pepper Hamilton investigation and Baylor University's failures regarding Title IX compliance. The document notes the following:

- "...the University as a whole failed to prioritize Title IX implementation."[15]

- "...Baylor lacked the sufficient infrastructure and an informed policy."[16]

- "In addition, as of the spring of 2015, there were no clear protocols for documentation or consistency in practice across implementers."[17]

- Trauma-based information was not considered.[18]

Included in the document is a discussion of the football program. Simply put, the program existed in an institution that insufficiently supported Title IX. Therefore, the program operated within an in-house system of investigation and discipline, not unlike that discussed in Luther's *Unsportsmanlike Conduct*. The "Findings of Fact" note that this system resulted in safety risks for the University and prevented implementation of Title IX.[19]

The institution-wide lack of Title IX compliance astounded me. The University made itself a powder keg looking for a match. How could an excellent school have glaring deficiencies in procedure? The lack of compliance for the campus permitted the creation of the culture found in the football program as well as the campus in general.

In the end, Baylor University's commitment is to education, not fundraising through football. Under the cover of a Christian environment, the campus commitment to help those who are injured and protect those who are vulnerable is a chance to live out the Christian values they claim to hold. Following the laws, including Title IX, for providing said education in a safe environment for all students must supersede any desire to field a winning football team that will in turn bring in more money for the school.

****

What About Your School?

When your alma mater's football team makes the news for all the wrong reasons, you get defensive (no pun intended) about the team and the school. One defensive tactic I witnessed on social media was the "What about (fill in school name here)?" Unfortunately, so many schools and their teams have their own cases of sexual and physical assault that a Baylor fan could place virtually any large school program in the blank.

I address this topic here because I want to let you, the reader, know: 1) I am not ducking the scope of the problem, and 2) Why I remain focused on Baylor.

1. The Scope of the Problem: During my research, I found names of other large schools with reports of sexual assault, including my alma mater, the University of Texas. For those of you who want to point and say, "What about Texas?" I reply, "Yes, it happened here as well." I do not know enough details of the cases and that's not the goal of this book, but I want Baylor fans to know that I am not turning a blind eye to my own school. I find sexual assaults on any campus tragic.

2. Why I focus on Baylor: My work discusses Baylor's cases because they grabbed my attention the most. I found Baylor's situation especially hurtful because of their Christian background. Those foundational values were absent in the way the survivors of sexual assault were treated. As a Christian, and a college football fan, the treatment of these women, who allege they were victims of crime, made me look at how Christians lose sight of being servants of Christ when we let wordly goals become our focus.

****

What Did Coach Briles Know?

It's okay to admit it: you flipped through the book to this chapter first, didn't you? It's the question everyone wants answered and the topic that still spawns social media arguments. Let's take a look at Art Briles and whether he played a role in the scandal or not.

Nick Eatman's book, *Friday, Saturday, Sunday in Texas*, found its way into my research stack during a library trip. The book was a gold mine in disguise.

Eatman chronicled football weekends in Texas: starting with Friday night high school games, through Saturday's college pageantry, and culminating with Sunday's professional games. Fortunately, the highlighted college team in this book happened to be Baylor. And the season just happened to be the 2015 season, when the news about the sex assaults surfaced.

The book got even better: Eatman's previous work includes a biographical work on Coach Art Briles. He knows Briles and the Briles family well. After I read through his work, I felt prepared to present a balanced view of the coach to you.

When his book was published in 2016, Eatman made a good case for Art Briles not playing a role in any sort of cover up for sexual assault. He doesn't make Briles a sympathetic character, in my opinion, but provides a picture to remind us all that – no matter what -- the coach is a human being with a family. It was only later that allegations of Briles' involvement in discouraging reporting of assaults, as well as text messages commenting on men who were alleged to have committed assaults, told a different side of the story.[20]

While the major Title IX trial won't begin until October 2019, enough of the plaintiffs' documents make me personally question the level of knowledge Briles had in some of the alleged events. Before Baylor Nation calls for my head on a platter, I reiterate: *these are plaintiffs' documents.* The reason a trial takes place is to test allegations -- and these allegations are no exception.

The plaintiffs' (Jane Doe 1-10) documents present, at a minimum, a culture hostile to women who reported alleged assaults. In addition, Baylor's failure as an institution to provide adequate support to survivors based on Title IX echoes conclusions from Pepper Hamilton's presentation.

Fairness in presenting this information remains a goal of this work. Therefore, I *want* to believe Briles was sincere in his letter to Baylor Nation dated June 2, 2016.[21] As a survivor supporter, I also believe the survivors who felt dissuaded by the football staff from reporting their assaults. By firing the coach, Baylor took a step forward in changing a culture that appears hostile to women who are courageous enough to report assault.

So, did Coach Briles know anything? He knew enough. Consider the concept that head coaches know "everything" going on with their program. They usually have an assistant, with the title of Director of Football Operations, who serves as a gatekeeper of sorts. If there's a problem with a player, the Director resolves it – until it becomes a big problem. At that point, the head coach learns of it. However, it's unlikely the Director keeps a coach in the dark, either.

Consider the now-dropped case of Colin Shillinglaw.

****

Author's Update on Art Briles

Imagine my surprise when, while writing this book, I found this article on Twitter. http://www.espn.com/college-football/story/_/id/22975930/baylor-bears-paid-former-football-coach-art-briles-151-million-ouster. Friends tweeted it and pasted it to my Facebook wall as well- they all know what I've worked on for so many months.

What does the article say? Simply stated, Art Briles received a $15.1 million settlement when he left Baylor. The university owed him $39 million, based on the contract in place at the time of his separation.

My thoughts ran along the lines of, *Oh my word. Seriously?* This payout happened after his firing in 2016, and represented half of what remained on his contract, according to the article. I found it surprising that he still sought coaching jobs despite this generous compensation.

One thing is certain: he's a tough man. He's overcome plenty of adversity in his life. (Remember, this is the man who lost both parents and an aunt in a car crash when he played for the University of Houston. His family was traveling to his game when the fatal accident occurred.) He will survive the negative media spotlight as well.

****

The Case of Colin Shillinglaw

One of the best sources for information about what Coach Briles might or might not have known comes from a lawsuit that was later dropped. Collin Shillinglaw served as Assistant Athletic Director for Football Operations for Briles. As mentioned previously, this is the "gatekeeper" to the coach who also solves smaller problems before they become big problems.

Shillinglaw, who worked with Briles at Stephenville High School in Stephenville, Texas, in the late 1980s and at the University of Houston, sued Baylor University, several members of the Board of Regents, and Pepper Hamilton for defamation in January 2017. He claimed he was unable to find employment after being fired from Baylor in May 2016, during the height of the scandal's media firestorm. (Note: Shillinglaw filed the suit in Dallas County court, not McLennan County, where Waco is located, because he lived in Dallas County at the time.)

The answer filed by the Board of Regents

members mentioned in the suit provided enough information to cast Shillinglaw in a more unfavorable light than even Briles, and likely led to the suit being dropped. While this case was never tried, the claims in the filings add depth to the scenario in place at Baylor during the Art Briles era.

Notably, in the introduction of the answer, the regents claim Shillinglaw's suit was "…intended to hide the truth about how Shillinglaw, Coach Briles and others created a culture within the football program that shielded players from University discipline…"[22] Further, this culture, in concert with Baylor's Title IX deficiencies at the time, "…led to reports of sexual assaults and other disciplinary problems involving football players being mishandled or not reported to appropriate Baylor personnel."[23]

Sounds pretty bad, doesn't it? Remember, this is the defense's answer to a defamation lawsuit, so the words need to sound tough. However, some claims that the defense lists as statements of fact, sound even worse than this introduction.

The Text Messages

According to the regents' answer, during the Pepper Hamilton investigation, they "…*found evidence that Briles relied on Shilinglaw to line up legal representation for players who had run-ins with the law.*"[24] As part of the non-reporting of disciplinary issues to appropriate Baylor personnel, the regents cited several text messages from Coach Briles:

An incident on April 8, 2011 where Briles texts "…*Just trying to keep him away from our judicial affairs folks…*" regarding a freshman player cited for illegal consumption of alcohol.[25]

An incident on September 30, 2013, where a player was arrested for assault; Briles texted the Athletics Director, *"(the player) said Waco PD was there-said they were going to keep it quiet...I'll get shill (sic) (Shillinglaw) to ck (sic) on Sibley (Waco area attorney Jonathan Sibley)."*[26]

These are only two examples out of several listed in the response. Unfortunately, they don't reflect well on Shillinglaw or Briles. The Board of Regents also found this evidence disconcerting, which ultimately led them to change the personnel in the program.

The Sexual Assaults

Another aspect of the response to the Shillinglaw claims stems from several claims of sexual assault by players. The Findings of Fact presented by Pepper Hamilton to the Board of Regents noted: *"In certain instances, including reports of a sexual assault by multiple football players, athletics and football personnel affirmatively chose not to report sexual violence and dating violence to an appropriate administrator outside of athletics."*[27]

To support this statement, the defense presented the following:

> *A female student alleging dating violence committed by Shawn Oakman, a transfer player from Penn State, filed a report with Waco Police on January 10, 2013. The woman claims she hand-delivered a copy of this police report to Collin Shillinglaw, as well as two other football personnel members, but no evidence exists that Shillinglaw or the other personnel presented*

*this report to anyone outside the Athletics
Department.*

*The student chose not to file charges and
left Baylor. On her return to Baylor during
the summer and fall semesters of 2013, she
ended up withdrawing from the university
because she ran into Oakman, who allegedly
assaulted her the first time they met, then
punched a hole in the wall the next time they
met.*[28]

Despite these alleged incidents, Oakman was
only suspended for the season opener in 2015. He
went on to play the rest of the season and graduated in
December 2015.

Unfortunately, he allegedly assaulted a student
on April 1, 2016. Currently, he is awaiting trial for that
incident.[29]

Remember, this is a synopsis of a synopsis from
a defense response to allegations. However, it begs the
question: *if Shillinglaw had reported Oakman the first
time, when he had a police report in hand, would the
April 1 incident have occurred?* We will never know for
sure.

The next incident presented by the defense
turned my stomach.

A female student-athlete alleged a gang rape by
five football players in early 2012. She told her coach,
who wrote down the names of the accused players,
then took the information to the Athletics Director, Ian
McCaw.[30] From there, AD McCaw told the woman's
coach to speak to Coach Briles. According to the
defense's response, based on the Pepper Hamilton

Findings of Fact, Briles' initial response was, *"Those are some bad dudes...Why was she around those guys?"[31]*

Let's look at that again. *"Those are some bad dudes?"* Really? This response minimizes the victim's assault at best. Even if one tries to give Coach Briles the benefit of the doubt, this is a terrible response.

Briles is alleged to have told the female athlete's coach that she needed to tell the police. This is good advice, but an extra effort to call the police as well would have been better. Suspending the players accused of the crime until further investigation would also show an effort to be fair in the face of an accusation. In the end, no one in Judicial Affairs or any other department outside Athletics received a report of this incident, according to Pepper Hamilton's investigation.[32]

The Athletics Department was not equipped to handle an investigation of alleged sexual assault. Baylor University did not provide clear procedures or protocols for reporting assault at that time. Consequently, incidents like this were not properly reported or investigated. Without an investigation, no proper disciplinary actions were meted out, either.

What Happened Next?

According to the regents' response, once all the Findings of Fact were presented by Pepper Hamilton, Coach Briles spoke to the Board of Regents.

Art Briles made an emotional statement to the board. He admitted making mistakes, and that he left discipline issues to his personnel instead of reporting them. By leaving his staff to manage disciplinary issues, he ran the risk of never knowing about them. The board asked him what changes he would make in running the program. He responded, "Tell me what you want to do and I'll do it."[33]

He did not promote an action plan for improving the management of disciplinary issues. According to the regents' response, they expected to hear action plans as well. Specifically, "The Board was concerned that given all that had occurred, Coach Briles could not identify with the role of disciplinarian."[34]

Coach Art Briles remains an outstanding coach. That can never be taken away from him. In the realm of collegiate athletics, however, the disciplinarian role is crucial. College athletes are young men who need guidance. With that in mind, the idea of Briles coaching on the collegiate level is not a good fit. Coaching on a professional level would not be out of the question for him, though.

Return to the original question: Did Coach Briles know?

As stated before, he knew enough. Perhaps the Title IX trial in 2019 will tell the public he knew more than is presented here. For now, I stand by saying he knew enough. It was, unfortunately, enough for him to be removed from his job.

It was also enough for several women to have their lives disrupted by the alleged assaults.

It Wasn't Just Football

During my review of the timeline of cases, I ran across the name of Jacob Anderson, the former President of Baylor's Phi Delta Theta fraternity chapter. Mr. Anderson was indicted on four counts of felony sexual assault in March 2017.[35]

This was a good reminder that Baylor's "problem" was not exclusive to the football team. *The Hunting Ground*, a moving documentary on campus sexual assault and Title IX violations, reports that while most sexual assaults on campus are committed by athletes, the next largest group of perpetrators is fraternity members. These men are also the most likely to become major donors after graduation, which gives them a quasi-shield from investigation like that given to athletes.[36]

Author's Update on Jacob Anderson

The Jacob Walter Anderson case took an astonishing turn while I completed this work. In October 2018, months after his trial was initially set to begin, Anderson took a plea bargain. His indictment read four counts of sexual assault, but in the plea deal he pleaded no-contest to the lesser count of unlawful restraint. Included in this plea are punishments of three years of deferred probation, a $400 fine, and counseling.

A statement from the victim's family appears in the article as well. They allege that they were not aware of any plea deal, and that despite the victim's reporting of the assault and getting an examination at the hospital, she did not receive justice. The line that stands out the most to me came from the victim's attorney: "It pays to be rich."

Source: https://www.wacotrib.com/news/courts_and_trials/former-baylor-fraternity-leader-accused-of-rape-pleads-to-lesser/article_608dd85e-0302-591c-a4f8-d55bc98a000d.html

The Victims-Remember Them?

Football players allegedly committing sexual assaults and alleged cover-ups of these events by their coach put Baylor in the headlines. Those headlines caught your eye, of course. Who doesn't want to watch a scandal unfold in the media?

Unfortunately, the focus on athletes and coaches took the attention away from the group who deserved the most support: the victims.

BEHIND THE JANE
DOE LABEL

"So God created man in his own image, in the image of God he created him; male and female he created them." Genesis 1:27 (ESV)

Here's a confession: I do not read the Bible enough. When I do read it, I do not always absorb it the way I should. I look over the word without thinking about what they mean, especially words like those above from Genesis. We "know" the creation story, don't we? No need to spend too much time on it, right?

When my pastor used the term *imago dei* ('image of God") in sermons, I started thinking about what it means. Then I returned to the creation story, and it made sense in a deeper way. *God made humankind in his image!* From there, I realized: crimes against people like murder, assault, and rape all destroy the image of God. Justin and Lindsey Holcomb put a finer point on it in their book, *Rid of My Disgrace:* "Simply put, when someone defaces a human being—God's image-bearer—ultimately an attack is being waged against God himself."[37]

I am not a Bible scholar, so forgive any holes in

my interpretation. However, my focus on attacks made on God's image-bearers in crimes like assault clarified their serious nature. These were women created in God's image, who were violated, regardless of who hurt them. A Christian university needed to keep that knowledge in mind once they learned of these assaults. The victims who were brave enough to report their trauma deserved compassion from their university, simply because they are made in God's image. Regrettably, Baylor failed to provide that compassion.

Ten of these survivors are the plaintiffs in a civil suit against Baylor for Title IX violations. Known as "Jane Doe 1-10", they sought, but did not receive, assistance from the university in the wake of experiencing a violent crime. That alleged lack of assistance provides the basis for their case. These women are not the only ones who sued Baylor in Title IX cases, but this case remains the largest one that has not been tried or settled.

What Are They Claiming?

The plaintiffs claim they were not informed of their rights under Title IX when they reported being sexually assaulted to different departments at Baylor. Based on the complaint filed by the plaintiffs, some specific claims include:

- (From Jane Doe 1) "The Defendant's physician (Note: an on-campus physician) mis-informed Jane Doe 1 and concealed from Jane Doe 1 as to her options to further report the incident, accommodations she was entitled to under Title IX, and further investigatory actions that could be taken by the University."[38]

- (From Jane Doe 2) "Jane Doe 2 also reported the incident to the Baylor Health Center personnel and a physical exam was performed, but no rape kit was prepared.[39]

- Jane Doe 2 was able to attend free counseling sessions at the University Counseling Center, but was forced to discontinue her sessions when advised that she had used up all of her allotted sessions, and therefore, would have to seek treatment elsewhere."[40] (Note: this claim is made by several of the Jane Does.)

- (From Jane Doe 5) "The counselor (Note: from the Baylor Counseling Center) advised Jane Doe 5 not to come forward (Note: to report the assault) for the stated reason that doing so would stress her out too much and instead she should focus on school.

- The counselor also advised that if Jane Doe 5 came forward, her friends, family and class mates would be made aware of the incident."[41]

Finally, from Jane Doe 7, who had a rape kit performed that confirmed forcible sexual intercourse:

"The assault occurred during finals. Jane Doe 7 requested accommodations from Defendant University and her professors directly that were all denied.

One professor told Jane Doe 7 that her sexual assault was not really assault."[42]

These claims provide enough information to see the survivors allege a dismissive attitude by Baylor resulting in serious infringements of their rights under Title IX. Each Jane Doe deserves the opportunity to sue Baylor for these alleged infringements and to have some sense of justice. Even though their lives are forever changed, their inner strength will prevail. I pray they will use this horrible chapter in their lives to build themselves into amazing women in their work, families, and communities.

The dismissive attitude from Baylor is more troubling in the context of Christian living. These women were neither heard nor believed, according to these allegations. Women made in the image of God. That's who these Jane Doe survivors are. Remember that, please. It's something that Baylor forgot.

WHAT I LEARNED ABOUT BAYLOR'S CAMPUS CULTURE

BAYLOR'S CAMPUS CULTURE

How could victims be ignored? Why didn't the school mention the number of assaults that non-athletes allegedly committed? An incomplete puzzle lay before me with a frustrating amount of missing pieces. When I remembered the survivors, who were facing a battle in court and the challenge of healing, it gave me the impetus to keep moving forward and try to find some of those missing pieces. From the outset, I accepted that I would not find everything I wanted to learn: the trial would be the source for most of the answers. In the meantime, I asked myself one crucial question: could I find something to explain *why* such a horrible amount of criminal behavior flew under the radar at a Christian school?

Plaintiffs' documents filed for the ten Jane Does provided the box of puzzle pieces to scan. Were there pieces to put together to outline the campus culture at Baylor? One clue we can consider is the deposition from Dr. David Garland, which shows an example of uninterested leadership at the university.

The David Garland Deposition

Baylor's Board of Regents named Dr. Garland the school's Interim President after Ken Starr left Baylor in May 2016. Prior to this appointment, Dr. Garland served as Dean of Truett Theological Seminary, Baylor's seminary. He also served as Interim President before the Regents hired Ken Starr. You would expect, then, that Dr. Garland knew the Baylor campus and administration. He was not a stranger to the school.

In his May 2017 deposition, however, he sounded as if he recently arrived on campus for the sole purpose of implementing the Pepper Hamilton recommendations -- as though he had no idea why he was being deposed – except he knew to answer questions about Pepper Hamilton's suggestions.

Here are a few examples. (Note: Questions (Q) are asked by the plaintiffs' attorney and answers (A) are given by Dr. Garland.)

"Q: Did you understand the subject matter that we were going to talk about today?...

A: I'm not fully aware what kind of questions you'll ask. I have a general idea that it would be about the sexual assaults that you're representing.

Q: And you are aware that we represent 10 young women who have brought claims that they were sexually assaulted, and it involves their treatment by the university. You're aware of that?

A: I'm aware that you represent them,

yes.

Q: And despite that, you sit here today, and you don't know anything about our clients' claims except one of them might have filed an appeal to you?

A: No, I do not.

Q: Are you not interested in it?

A: I am always interested in victims, but – who are becoming survivors, but I don't know their individual cases."[43]

The fact that Dr. Garland didn't learn about the cases does not match up to the claim of being "interested in victims." While these questions came from the plaintiffs' attorneys, the air of nonchalance about the safety of the students entrusted to Baylor poses a challenge for the defense once the trial starts. Overall, the lack of concern from a Christian school makes the exchange more incredible.

In his testimony, Dr. Garland emphasized that his main purpose as Interim President was to implement the recommendations from Pepper Hamilton -- which he completed. Setting up processes and protocols where none previously existed sounds like a major accomplishment. However, how much help will such processes provide if the attitude of the campus is as dismissive as Dr. Garland's?

Buddy Jones's Email

Reports of former Baylor Regent Neal "Buddy"

Jones's emails hit the papers in July 2017. He creatively referred to a group of young women who were depicted drinking alcohol as "perverted little tarts."[44] (Note: The young women Jones references were *not* assault victims.) This article shows the mindset of an authority figure at Baylor. If this was the mentality of a Baylor regent during the years these assaults occurred, and women sought help from the university, no wonder they couldn't find it.

Considering Jones's mindset from a Christian perspective brings the following Bible verse to mind: "For out of the abundance of the heart the mouth speaks." Matthew 12:34 (ESV) What does this say about the attitude of a leader at a Christian university? How many other "godly" men in positions of leadership share this mentality about young women who drink? Hopefully, truly "godly" men, particularly those in university leadership, find this "perverted little tart" mentality archaic and unacceptable in the twenty-first century.

Idolatry

Baylor's rise in the national spotlight, due in part to the football team's success, provided a fork in the road for their leadership: to continue in their mission of education based on Christian principles, or to move in a new direction seeking the worldly status, and more money, from their football success. They traded their faith for worldly gain, a modern golden calf idol that, you might say, resembles a Heisman trophy. In the process of making this change, they swept a major problem, campus sexual assault, under the carpet. When Baylor made this choice, the consequence of not addressing the problem in the interest of maintaining its reputation was that women suffered from these violent crimes.

Justin and Lindsay Holcomb provide a sound explanation of idolatry and violence in their book, *Rid of My Disgrace: Hope and Healing for Victims of Sexual Assault,* a helpful work on healing from sexual assault from a Christian perspective:

"After the fall, humankind was enslaved to idolatry (hatred for God) and violence (hatred for each other)...Idolatry is not the ceasing of worship. Rather, it is *misdirected worship,* and at *the core of idolatry is self-worship.*"[45] (Author's emphasis)

Level with me: did that hurt a little to read? The conviction I felt in my spirit when I read that sentence made me say, "Oh, wow!" out loud.

Misdirected worship. That's when we do the "Benediction Shuffle" out of the sanctuary to catch the kickoff of our NFL team's game during the final hymn. Those not-so-subtle steps out of the sanctuary means you feel bad about leaving a little early, but the Cowboys play at noon, for heaven's sake! (Full disclosure: I've shuffled a few times and even wore a Rob Gronkowski jersey to church the day the Patriots played the Cowboys.)

When we care too much about our college team's success, we also fall to misdirected worship. A stunning example of this "misdirected worship" came from the Board of Regents' response to the now-dropped Colin Shillinglaw lawsuit.

Despite learning from the "Findings of Fact" about the violence allegedly committed by football players, some of the major donors still wanted to keep

Coach Briles at Baylor. After all, Briles turned the program around - from laughingstock to formidable - and Baylor football's future looked bright. These donors met with a group of regents seeking specific details of evidence that led the Board of Regents to make changes regarding Coach Briles's employment. The regents did not disclose those details for privacy reasons.

When the regents noted that keeping the leadership that allowed so many failings in the Title IX policies would not "uphold the 'mission of the University,'" they received a surprising response from an undisclosed donor we will call -- "Donor X."[46]

Donor X allegedly responded to the regents, "If you mention Baylor's mission one more time, I'm going to throw up...I was promised a national championship."[47]

Yes, this response was allegedly made by a donor to a Baptist university.

At the core of idolatry is self-worship. By giving money to build Baylor football into a national championship level program, Donor X would have the satisfaction not only of bragging about his school's win, but also of knowing he helped, in his own way, make it possible. Ask yourself: *Was Donor X's motivation to glorify God or himself?* We will never know the answer, but if Donor X wanted a national championship more than he wanted Baylor to fulfill its mission, a viable argument for *self-worship* exists.

Sports idolatry easily leads to self-worship. We want others to perceive us as winners. When *our* team wins, *we* win, don't we? The euphoria of victory makes us dizzy, and in our celebration, we act as though WE scored the winning points. The next day at work, we behave obnoxiously and make sure to walk by the desk of the co-worker who trash talked our team the previous week. Self-worship, much?

The Biggest Piece of the Puzzle

The *Waco Tribune*'s Phillip Ericksen broke the story that shed the most light on Baylor's campus culture in a June 27, 2018, article. Ericksen reported that former Athletics Director, Ian McCaw, gave a deposition to the plaintiffs' attorneys in the Title IX case with the ten Jane Does.[48] If McCaw's name sounds familiar, it's because he was referenced earlier as allegedly learning of a gang rape committed by five football players.

McCaw currently serves as Director of Athletics at Liberty University, a Christian university seeking to upgrade its reputation in sports (sound familiar?). McCaw provided detailed testimony of his time at Baylor. The Ericksen article provides a comprehensive overview, but I read the deposition as well for further clarification.

Regarding the alleged report of a gang rape:

"Q: Have you ever received any information about an alleged gang rape involving student athletes?

A: I received information about a sexual assault. I was never told of a gang rape.

Q: You've seen that since you left the university, at least, reported in the media?

A: Yeah. The regents seem to like to use that term.

Q: Do you have any sense of why that's so?

A: I think to inflame the scandal."[49]

McCaw's claim to not have this information could make the trial interesting. As the questioning moves on, McCaw repeats his overall view on what happened at Baylor several times. The following question and response say it best:

"Q: So (sic) we'll obviously get into your departure from the university and that of Coach Briles, but is it your belief that you were made to be a scapegoat?

A: Principally Coach Briles was made to be a scapegoat. I think I was probably in the wrong place at the wrong time."[50]

You know by now I am hardly an Art Briles fan, but I found this characterization of him interesting. It fits in with what McCaw further claims in his testimony, such as this question and response:

"Q: All right. The next person you mentioned was Mr. Willis (a regent). What information did you gather that gave you concern that he bears some responsibility (regarding Title IX issues)?

A: I think he was the main conspirator in putting together this elaborate plan that essentially scapegoated the black football players and the football program for being responsible for what was a decades-long, university-wide sexual assault scandal."[51]

Scapegoating athletics and athletes, particularly black football players, to cover up a campus-wide sexual assault problem. Was this Baylor's campus culture? Was this why no one seemed to realize a serious problem with sexual assaults on campus existed? If the Board of Regents attempted to hide the amount of assaults by focusing on the few cases that made headlines because they involved football players, then minimizing the trauma of the victims and not providing the supports they deserved according to Title IX made sense.

It made sense, but still resulted in adding to the trauma the women, who allege they were ignored by the university when they sought help, already faced.

The three-hundred-and-fifty-page deposition of Ian McCaw includes many details, including that he believes that the "Findings of Fact" were written by a few regents with the intent of skewing the data to make the football program look bad.[52]

He also claims he was unaware of any procedure for reporting sexual assault to the university from 2003 to September 2014[53], and that the student code of conduct was "sometimes lax" regarding sexual assault and interpersonal violence.[54]

Overall, Ian McCaw's deposition provided the most insight to the inner workings of Baylor University.

After my deep dive into stacks of documents, what did I conclude?

CHOOSING FAITH
OVER FOOTBALL

CHOOSING FAITH
OVER FOOTBALL

In researching the Baylor story, I found a campus that sacrificed the safety of its students to maintain its reputation. Football players were not the only alleged perpetrators of assault, either. The media focused on the football players for the best headlines, but non-athletes allegedly assaulted women as well. Consequently, the survivors alleging assaults by non-athletes – who do not have the flashy stories for the media-- fade into the background more than the survivors of alleged assaults by football players. But guess what? They were just as hurt, just as devastated, and just as ignored by Baylor as any woman who was hurt by a football player.

Enough material exists to write another book on how the mainstream and social media handled this story. What happens in this media escapade is that the lives of real people are forgotten as the story is told and re-told. At Baylor, survivors of violent crimes found themselves in the media spotlight with their lives' darkest moments provided to the public for its consumption.

The Ian McCaw deposition gives us the best illustration, to date, of the prevailing culture of Baylor's leadership. The purposeful deflection of the breadth of the campus assault issue to focus on the alleged assaults committed by football players, combined with the lack of Title IX procedures and minimizing of the victims' needs, led to a toxic atmosphere for students. The machinations alleged in McCaw's deposition show us a university that moved off the path of living out the Christian values it claimed to espouse.

In the end, the questions of which coaches knew about assaults and whether they tried to cover them up distract us from the heart of the problem at Baylor, the campus culture set by its Board of Regents. The regents rode the financial and media success generated by the football team's turnaround onto the path away from its humble beginnings as an institution founded on Christian principles.

Throw the yellow flag for interference, sports fan. This campus leadership interfered with the victims, now survivors, who attempted to access the help they were supposed to receive from that same leadership.

Throw the yellow flag for interference again. The drive for material success interfered with the fundamental purpose of Baylor University: to provide excellent education in a safe environment reflecting the principles of the Christian faith.

Throw the yellow flag...on *us* as sports fans. We need to quit putting athletes on a pedestal. Eighteen- to twenty-year-old kids do not possess the maturity to handle the attention they are given. We need to stop thinking coaches walk on water, too. In short, we need to not idolize any of these men. They are human, and they will make mistakes. If we continue to worship them, they will believe the rules do not apply to them.

Based on what we've learned about sports and violence, criminal consequences result from that mindset. Do not let your daughter, sister, or friend be what these men choose to take because they believe they can.

The legal cases that make it to trial will give me the chance to sort out the truth. I want to hear the other side, because what I hear from the survivors horrifies me. How does the university defend this behavior? I plan to attend as many days in court as I can to hear Baylor's explanation.

You know what made me the most angry? The use of the word "tarts" by Buddy Jones. As a reminder, the women he described with this moniker were NOT women involved in any of the assaults, but female students drinking in celebration of a friend's engagement. In any event, labeling women as "tarts" for drinking is every single evangelical Christian stereotype multiplied by ten. I hurt for the women at Baylor, if that is the kind of person who sits in governance over their university.

Women do not stand any chance of a fair hearing if that is the attitude expressed by the leadership. An attitude that a woman is a "tart" for drinking leads to other clichéd expressions such as, "She was asking for it," or "What was she wearing?" *(Note: Jones is no longer a Regent at Baylor.)*

Understand me here, please: I am not saying it's a good idea to go out and get drunk every weekend when you are in college. Far from it. I am saying, that when you are drinking and if you are assaulted, it is not automatically your fault just because you were drinking. The women who were intoxicated when they were assaulted did not want to be assaulted.

Ladies, here's the other side of that: if people out there will think you are a "tart" for drinking, you will have a hard time being heard and believed if you are assaulted. I hate that for you, but it's the truth. Do not let that stop you from reporting. If you are assaulted, report it. Be brave, you have that strength in you.

Until our society loses the attitude of "tarts" drinking, it's incumbent on those of us who care for survivors to do all we can to help change that mindset. Responsibility lies with women *and* men in preventing sexual assault on any campus. Yes, a woman does well to keep track of how much alcohol she drank, but a man does well to not see a woman impaired by alcohol and think she is an easy target.

I learned more about college football than I ever cared to during this endeavor. However, in this quest for the truth, I reached the other side with my faith not only intact but stronger. I learned to look past the *interference* of worldly goals to find the Cross, where my eyes need to remain fixed but where I often forget to focus. I enjoy college football still but with renewed perspective: it is a game. The real battle occurs off the field, as I walk out my daily life surrendering to Christ.

My prayer is for Baylor's renewed commitment to student safety to include centering its goals on Christ. By returning to the ultimate foundation of the school, the university finds true victory, regardless of the football team's win-loss record.

My prayer is for Christians who enjoy watching sports to ask themselves if their attitude toward sports is healthy. Have you made sports an idol in your life? Are you finding your identity in your alma mater and the prowess of their football team, or are you remembering your identity is in Christ? I confess I misplaced my priorities and allowed college football to take over a place where only Christ belongs in my life. Have you done the same thing? If so, I challenge you to remember who really belongs at the Number One ranking every season, regardless of whom the College Football Playoff committee selects.

ABOUT FALSE REPORTING

FALSE REPORTING

"You shall not bear false witness against your neighbor." Exodus 20:16 (ESV)

Did you know false reporting of sexual assault occurred in the Bible? In Genesis chapter 39, Joseph turns down the advances of his boss's wife on more than one occasion. She tries one more time to proposition Joseph and grabs his outer garment as she speaks to him. Joseph runs away, leaving the garment in her hands. She uses this garment as proof that he tried to rape her -- she claimed she screamed and he ran away, leaving his garment behind. Joseph found himself in prison after this false accusation. Simply stated, false reporting is not a new concept.

While false accusations do not play a role in the Baylor story (to the best of my knowledge), discussing false reports brings balance to the conversation on sexual assault. The statistics remain low for false reporting: according to the National Sexual Violence Resource Center, the rate is between 2% and 10%.[55] Unfortunately, men facing false accusations experience their own challenges while proving their innocence.

The Duke lacrosse case shows the harsh realities

that false accusations may involve. Have you watched "Fantastic Lies," the ESPN special that discusses the Duke case? If not, do me a favor and watch it after you finish this book. That documentary scared the hell out of me as a mother of sons. I teared up along with the players' moms. I wanted to reach out and hug them. The pain they suffered watching their sons' reputations ruined by false accusations was palpable.

Duke was an unusual situation. The film walks you through that. Too many elements combined to create a perfect storm: the "rich, white boys" playing the quintessential rich, white boy sport at a premier university versus the poor woman of color who lived in town and was hired to service their sexual needs; the district attorney who found a way to coast to re-election, or so he thought; the media turning up the spotlight to destroy these falsely accused men as a disgusting display of (white) male privilege. And what was the result? A chaotic scene where young men were put in a situation in which they did not belong. The accuser, a troubled young woman, continued a downward spiral in her life (if you don't know where she is now, watch the film). The district attorney, who appeared troubled in his own right, ruined more lives than his with his zeal to win his campaign.[56]

In the end, no one won.

The numbers for false reporting may be small, but to a man falsely accused of a serious crime, that small percentage does not matter. As an advocate for survivors of sexual assault, and a mother of two sons, I draw this conclusion: women do not deserve to be sexually assaulted, and men do not deserve to be falsely accused of sexual assault.

ACKNOWLEDGMENTS

You hold in your hands the results of two years of work. I read, re-read and eventually wrote. I took a few long breaks to recover emotionally from what I read. Many people helped me on the journey. If I forget to name you here, I apologize.

My husband, Jay, deserves more thanks than I can bestow. He believed in my capabilities and encouraged me when my heart felt heavy from writing on such an intense subject. Thank you, my beloved, for everything. My sons, John and Noah: thank you for being quiet while Mommy wrote "her football book," and making me laugh with your entertaining antics when I needed to take a break. You are my sunshine and my laughter.

Becca Lower, from LowerTheBoom Editing, check it out, lady! We did it! Thank you so much for your patience with my mercurial self. You were the midwife as I birthed this book.

My church family at Redeemer Bible Church in Dallas: your prayers and interest in this work sustained me. I'm blessed to have you for prayer warriors.

Mary DeMuth and my fellow authors from Mary's July 2017 Intensive: thank you for your support and great ideas. Love and blessings to each of you.

My Twitter family: Aggie, AJ, Beaker, Bone, Brian, Brick, Dan, Diane, Donna, G, Hammy, Jodi, Katie, Kurt, Lu, RW, Stacey, Stan, Tina; y'all have been there from idea to reality. You've encouraged me and listened to me gripe along the way. Love "all y'all!"

My podcast family: Matt Davidson, Marc and Vicci Henry, Dan Kueck; so proud of the work we do together!

Sports guys who thought this would be a good project: Mark Lane, Mark Schofield, Mike Loveall, Kevin Lindstrom. Thank you!

Ole Miss Evie: thank you for your support on this project! Hotty Toddy!

David Walker, the Gentleman QB: thank you for your kindness, sir!

Celina Summers, you are da bomb. Thanks for everything!

To my Alpha Delta Pi sisters: thank you for reminding me that it's not just four years-it's a lifetime! Amanda, thank you for loaning me your condo so I could grab some solo writing time. Julia, thank you for being there for me then and now. Lauren, you remind me that I can do anything. Elizabeth, thank you for hosting me and letting me chatter while you patiently drank your coffee. Clair, shout out to my Big Sis! Love to each of you.

Erica Ogletree: I am grateful for your mentorship and to be a part of Sidelines and Pearls! Let's make some noise!

My "young guns" who liked this idea and let me run it by them as I moved forward on the project: Clara, Becca, Emma, Simon. Big hugs from Mrs. M! Lily and MK: thank you for watching the kids!

My parents, Bill and Laura Farmer and Little Brother, Steve Farmer: thank you for your love and support. I love y'all!

Ann Fleming: you are the best surrogate mom a girl could have. I love you!

Mrs. Passmore: Thank you for calling me a writer when I was too scared to believe it was a possibility.

Cindy Karm: I'm so grateful to have you in my life. You know all the old stories and remain my friend anyway!

Highest praises to Jesus Christ for redeeming my life. I pray this work glorifies You.

END NOTES

ENDNOTES

1 Jessica Luther and Dan Solomon, "Silence at Baylor," Texas Monthly, August 20, 2015, https://www.texasmonthly.com/article/silence-at-baylor.

2 ESPN (Television), "Allegations of Indifference at Baylor," Outside the Lines, http://www.espn.com/video/clip?id=14675314.

3 Jeff Benedict and Armen Keteyian, The System: The Glory and Scandal of Big-Time College Football (New York: Anchor Books, 2014), p. 197.

4 Kristi Dosh, Saturday Millionaires: How Winning Football Builds Winning Colleges (Nashville: Turner Publishing Company, 2013), Location 3810 on Kindle.

5 Ibid.

6 Ibid.

7 Ibid, Location 3865 on Kindle.

8 Ibid, Location 3907 on Kindle.

9 Ibid, Location 3953 on Kindle.

10 Ibid, Location 3974 on Kindle.

11 Ibid, Location 4088 on Kindle.

12 Jessica Luther, Unsportsmanlike Conduct: College Football and the Politics of Rape (New York: Edge of Sports c/o Akashic Books, 2016), p. 84.

13 Since the initial filings, an additional five Jane Does were added to this suit, which now reads Jane Doe 1-15. For this book, I only used information from the earlier filings.

14 Luther and Solomon.

15 Baylor University Board of Regents, "Findings of Fact," May 26, 2016, https://www.baylor.edu/thefacts/doc.php/266596.pdf, pg. 4.

16 Ibid.

17 Ibid, pg. 6.

18 Ibid, pg. 7.

19 Ibid, pg. 10

20 Sarah Mervosh, "Damning Texts Between Ex-Baylor Coach Briles, Other Officials Revealed in New Court Records," Dallas Morning News, February 2, 2017, https://www.dallasnews.com/news/baylor/2017/02/02/ex-baylor-coach-art-briles-officials-tried-hide-misconduct-football-players-court-record-shows.

21 Nick Eatman, Friday, Saturday, Sunday in Texas: A Year in the Life of Lone Star Football, from High School to College to the Cowboys (New York: Dey Street Books, 2016), pp. 337-338.

22 Colin Shillinglaw v. Baylor University, et al, Cause No: DC-17-01225 (Def.'s Gray, Murff, and Harper's Original Answer to Pls.' Original Petition 2).

23 Ibid.

24 Ibid, pg. 13.

25 Ibid.

26 Ibid, pg. 14.

27 Ibid, pg. 15.

28 Ibid, pg. 19.

29 Ibid, pg. 20.

30 Ibid.

31 Ibid, pg. 21.

32 Ibid, pp. 21-22.

33 Ibid, pg. 26.

34 Ibid, pg. 27.

35 Tommy Witherspoon, "Former Baylor Fraternity President Indicted in Sexual Assault," Waco Tribune-Herald, May 11, 2016, https://www.wacotrib.com/news/higher_education/former-baylor-fraternity-president-indicted-in-sexual-assault/article_54f53426-2847-504e-814f-f9fdabc2bd69.html.

36 The Hunting Ground, Directed by Kirby Dick, The Weinstein Company, Radius-TWC, February 27, 2015. https://www.amazon.com/Hunting-Ground-Kirby-Dick/dp/B014TVGEIW/ref=sr_1_1?ie=UTF8&qid=1550201979&sr=8-

1&keywords=the+hunting+ground

37 Justin S. Holcomb and Lindsey A. Holcomb, Rid of My Disgrace: Hope and Healing for Victims of Sexual Assault (Wheaton: Crossway, 2011), pg. 164.

38 Doe 1 et al v. Baylor University, Cause Number: 6:16-cv-00173-RP-JCM (Pls.' Third Am. Original Complaint and Jury Demand) Document 56, pg. 15.

39 Ibid, pg. 18.

40 Ibid, pp. 18-19.

41 Ibid, pg. 27.

42 Ibid, pg. 31.

43 Doe 1 et al v. Baylor University, (Garland Deposition) Document 106-1, pp. 11:8-12:2.

44 Matthew Watkins and Jim Malewitz, "As Baylor Regent, Lobbyist Called Drinking Female Students 'Perverted Little Tarts,'" Fort Worth Star-Telegram, July 2, 2017, http://www.star-telegram.com/news/state/texas/article159336959.html.

45 Holcomb and Holcomb, pg. 163.

46 Colin Shillinglaw v. Baylor University, et al, Cause No: DC-17-01225 (Def.'s Gray, Murff, and Harper's Original Answer to Pls.' Original Petition) pg. 28.

47 Ibid.

48 Phillip Ericksen, "McCaw: Baylor Regents Displayed Racism, Preferred Misleading Report

on Rape Scandal," Waco Tribune-Herald, June 27, 2018, https://www.wacotrib.com/news/higher_education/mccaw-baylor-regents-displayed-racism-preferred-misleading-report-on-rape/article_d6017176-142e-582d-a3bd-98c4a8e46e02.html.

49 Doe 1 et al v. Baylor University, Cause Number: 6:16-cv-00173-RP-JCM (McCaw Deposition) Document 438-1, p. 73:6-16. Note: This document number is according to the numbering of the complete filing, not the number on the deposition itself.

50 Ibid, pp. 73:24-74:5.

51 Ibid, p. 78:13-22.

52 Ibid, pp. 79-82.

53 Ibid, p. 215: 7-11.

54 Ibid, p. 221:14-22.

55 National Sexual Violence Resource Center, https://www.nsvrc.org/statistics.

56 Fantastic Lies, Directed by Marina Zenovich, ESPN Films, March 20, 2016. https://www.amazon.com/ESPN-Films-30-Fantastic-Lies/dp/B01D5GVBBM.

AFTERWORD

AFTERWORD

AFTERWORD

This journey through the saga at Baylor took me on a paper trail. I looked at news articles, primarily from the Waco Herald-Tribune, and documents filed for the upcoming Title IX trial for the ten (now fifteen) Jane Does.

I also learned about the lives of some of the women themselves, but in the interest of their privacy, that information remains off the record. They have been through enough with their experience, which is documented in the court records, and I did not want to further injure them.

I gave this project to God, to hopefully show all of us what can happen if we idolize sports and the people involved with the game. No one needed this lesson more than I did. I still enjoy watching sports, and seeing my team win, but the level of "hate" for opponents subsided from where it was at the start of this project. Once I understood that heaven will include Baylor Bears, Texas Longhorns, Texas A&M Aggies, and even (Lord help us!) University of Southern California Trojans, the game took a healthy place in my life instead of an all-consuming one.

CASE UPDATE ON SHAWN OAKMAN

UPDATE ON SHAWN OAKMAN'S CASE

Former football star Shawn Oakman's criminal trial in Waco took place as this book was in the final production stages. Verdict: not guilty of sexual assault. I include this information to make the book accurate. The verdict reminds us of the difficulty in trying and convicting sexual assault cases. The survivor filed a report, had a rape kit administered, and in short, did everything she was "supposed" to do in these situations. However, the burden of proof was not met according to the jury. Oakman will try to have a professional football career.

Source: https://www.wacotrib.com/news/courts_and_trials/jury-finds-former-baylor-football-player-oakman-not-guilty-of/article_ccb8e048-1d88-5a3c-a4c9-0adf5c080532.html

ABOUT LAURA LEIGH MAJERNIK

Seventh-generation Texan Laura Leigh Majernik debuts as an author with the release of Interference. A lifelong resident of Dallas, she fell in love with football under the "Friday Night Lights" as a third grader. In junior high school, she pretended to be a sports announcer as she made the school announcements, so it's no surprise to anyone who knows her that the subject of her first book is football. Laura Leigh blogs for SidelinesandPearls. com and serves as the Executive Producer for the Top Texas Prospects high school sports podcast. She lives in Dallas with her husband, Jay, two sons, and two dogs.